To Paul
a new but
special frei
With love.
from
ENJOY!

21 Days to ThanksLiving

Discovering the Power
of a Thankful Life

Dennis W. Dohner, PhD
Kristine Dohner

Published by:
Dennis W. Dohner & Kristine Dohner
The Family Church, 1529 Eureka Road, Roseville, CA 95661
dwdohner@gmail.com   kristinedohner@gmail.com

This publication is for general information purposes only. The methods
and content within this book are the authors' thoughts. They are not
intended to be a definitive set of instructions. This book contains information that is intended to help readers be better informed regarding a thankful lifestyle. While we try to keep the information up-to-date and correct,
there are no promises and or guaranties expressed or implied.

Scripture quotations are taken from:

The Holy Bible, Revised English Bible, (REB), copyright Oxford Press and
Cambridge University Press 1989

The Holy Bible, New International Version, (NIV), Copyright 1973, 1978,
1984, 2011, Biblica, Inc.

The Holy Bible, New Living Translation, (NLT) Copyright 1996, by Tyndale
Charitable Trust

All scriptures are NIV unless otherwise indicated.

ISBN-10: 197802665X
ISBN-13: 978-1978026650

Why This Book?

Thank You, God.

Thank You, God.

Thank You, God.

Thank You, God... No really... Thank You, for all that You have done.

Thank You, God...that I woke up today.

Thank You, God... for everything that I have.

Thank You, God... that You love me.

Thank You, God.

We wrote this book because we know ThanksLiving will change your life, as it has changed our lives. Being thankful is not something we do naturally, but is something we can learn to do all the time.

Thank You, God, for the ability to be thankful and that being thankful allows everything in our lives to be better!

It does take practice to say "Thank You" more than once.

Did you get tired after the second "Thank You, God," and then by the third one start to check out? That is not surprising. But once you truly understand the power of ThanksLiving, you will start to say, "Thank You, God" all the time. When you do... get ready for an amazing life!

21 Days to ThanksLiving

Table of Contents

Preface

In 2016, we were challenged to come up with an 18-day devotional on thankfulness that would lead up to Thanksgiving Day. In doing so, we discovered that while we were both very thankful for so much, there were many things to be grateful for that we had not really considered. Each of our lives have been filled with difficulties we would have preferred for someone else to live through instead of us. But in looking back, we are both grateful to not only have survived the challenges, but also to have learned what we did about God and ourselves through those seemingly impossible circumstances. This book is an opportunity to share with you what we now know about being thankful and to help you develop the life-changing attribute of ThanksLiving - living a lifestyle of gratitude.

Dennis

In 1985, I was diagnosed with my first heart problem. One of the major arteries was blocked 100% and I should have died. I did not, and for that I am very grateful. For me, this health crisis began the start of a journey of learning to be aware of the things in my life for which I should give thanks. I am thankful every day I wake up because I live in my extra days.

In America, our Thanksgiving Day is a great time to look back and consider all the things we are thankful for. I started, as many others, being thankful on that day, but not necessarily thankful for the gift of every day. Facing my own mortality changed how I began look at life, facing the mortality of a loved one changed it even more.

My late wife was diagnosed with a hidden, fast-growing breast cancer and given 12-18 months to live. I decided to have a very serious conversation with God about this. I had several questions, and of course, "Why?" was one of them. During this conversation, God shared a couple great truths with me that changed my world. The first truth was that neither my wife nor I were promised our next breath; each breath is an unearned gift. My job was to be thankful for those breaths and celebrate them each and every day, not just one day a year.

The next truth God shared with me was that "Why?" is the wrong question. The correct question is "Who?" *Who* was I going to believe, *who* was I going to trust and, most importantly, *who* was I going to *be* in the midst of a circumstance I really did not like? This challenge helped me begin to be thankful for each day that I have. Since then, I start each day with "Thank You, God! I woke up! It's going to be a great day because I am alive. Thank You, God, for all that You have done and are going to do."

Through the practice of thanking God every day I became more thankful for every little thing. The more I let thankfulness into my heart, the better I felt, and I could see more things to be thankful for. In studying the scriptures, I have found several keys to the Kingdom of God. *One is entering His gates with thanksgiving and into His courts with praise.* (Psalm 100:4) Since I wanted more of God, I continued thanking Him for everything. ThanksLiving is now a daily part of who I am. And it all started in the midst of a difficult time.

Once, a relative of mine was reading her Bible when God highlighted this verse in Philippians: *Rejoice in the Lord always. I will say it again: Rejoice!* (Philippians 4:4, NIV) She was conflicted and said, "No, I cannot rejoice in all things. I have a daughter who drinks too much. I can't be thankful for that." He would not let her get away from this verse, so finally, in great disgust and sarcasm, she prayed, "Thank you, God, for my daughter who drinks too much. But You know that. Thank you, God, for my daughter who is an alcoholic." After saying that prayer, begrudgingly, every day for a couple of weeks, the prayers began to change! "Thank you, Lord, for my daughter who has a drinking problem. You love her. Thank you, Lord, for my daughter who is still alive."

As her prayers changed, from disgust and sarcasm to sincere thankfulness and hope, so did her attitude. She began to be truly thankful that she had a daughter, who was still alive, which meant there was hope! Not too long after, she got a phone call from her daughter: she had checked herself into a rehab clinic and had found Jesus there. Being thankful and rejoicing in all things invites God to do what He does best – He brings clarity, hope, miracles, power, and victory!

Kristine

I first became aware of the power of thankfulness when my kids were young. For many years, I struggled with depression. I loved my family and knew I had a fairly good life, but felt daily like I lived in a black hole. The days all seemed to blend together in a dark cloud of unending feeding, diaper changing, corralling toys, meal preparation, cleanup, and the daunting task of just keeping four children alive.

One year, at a holiday craft fair, I found a stuffed fabric heart that bore the inscription, "The best remedy for discontentment is a thankful heart." This small heart hung in my kitchen over the sink to remind me that thankfulness had the power to overcome dark feelings. When I would have a difficult day, I began to thank God out loud for my husband, children, health, food in our cupboard, home, and for friends–those things that were obvious or felt like blessings. Every time I did this, I could feel the shift–a lightening–first in my heart, then in the atmosphere of my home.

During those times I learned that while I may not have control over my circumstances, I always have complete control over my attitude and responses. As I have grown in gratitude, I can now take thankfulness one step further and thank God not only for those things that *feel* worthy of thanks, but also for trials, illness, closed doors, betrayals, disappointments and failures. That sounds strange, but what I know about God's goodness is this: He is not the author of the bad thing–ever. Second, He is in the midst of whatever I am going through, walking with me and will, by my invitation, redeem all things. *And we know in all things God works for the good of those who love Him, who have been called according to His purpose.* Romans 8:28

Without fail, when I have given thanks not just in the face of adversity, but *for* the adversity, it diffuses hopelessness, anxiety, fear, anger, and depression, and releases positive, hopeful thoughts and feelings that bring about a more positive outcome. This release of supernatural grace brings incredible freedom in the spirit. Adverse situations have not taken me out of the game. They have stretched me, grown me, increased my compassion for the hurting, and given me a healthier skill set to deal with people and life. ThanksLiving has trained me to gaze at God and glance at my circumstances, rather than gaze at my circumstances and only glance at God.

My kids got to learn thankfulness too. When they were still young, no matter what I cooked, there was always someone who didn't like it. I decided the best way to remedy the daily complaining was to give my kids a "real world" experience. I explained that a bowl of rice, sometimes with a little protein, was the daily diet of much of the world. So, for the next two weeks, they were only going to eat rice and beans for every meal. It was a miracle! I never heard a complaint about the food again. Instead, they were thankful for whatever was placed on the table. You are never too young or too old to learn ThanksLiving.

"Gratitude unlocks the fullness of life. It turns what we have into enough, and more. It turns denial into acceptance, chaos to order, confusion to clarity. It can turn a meal into a feast, a house into a home, a stranger into a friend." - *Melody Beattie*

Introduction

Living in this world, with all its messiness and trials, can be difficult. We have learned that when you are thankful, your life gets better. What you are facing may not change, but when you become thankful your view of your circumstances improves. This *21 Days of ThanksLiving* daily devotional is designed to help you discover a simple way to live a better life.

You are what you feed on. In this book we are going suggest that you fill up and feed on thankfulness. As in most Kingdom principles, it is a lot easier than you think. The Psalmist, in 100:4 said, *Enter His gates with thanksgiving – and into His courts with praise.* These are not just good lyrics. Thanksgiving and praise are Kingdom keys that unlock the abundance that Jesus promised to you. Living a lifestyle of gratitude is ThanksLiving. For some, this shift is drastic and will take time and practice. This devotional is 21 days because it takes a minimum of three weeks to change how you see yourself, so that you can then establish a solid base for a new habit.

It is not always easy to give thanks, but it is something we must do in order to see God's best accomplished in our lives. It is how we move into higher realms of faith for ourselves, our family, our city, and for our nation. You may not be grateful by nature, but experts say gratitude is something you can learn. Even just thinking about being grateful can make you more grateful.

Spiritually, thanksgiving has great power to bring joy and break the power of the enemy. Whenever you give thanks to God, despite the most difficult circumstances, the enemy loses a big battle in your life. When you are thankful, your circumstances do not define you; they are just circumstances. When you give thanks in the midst of difficulty, you bring pleasure to God's heart. He is looking for people who live in a realm of praise and thanksgiving where the enemy no longer has an ability to hold or manipulate that person. Satan is defeated when you have a thankful heart because thankfulness during difficulty is a sacrifice pleasing to God. In fact, it is the love language of Heaven.

When we operate in a place of gratitude, we speak to the heart of God–the core of His character. We know that God is love, and gratitude is the expression of love. Salvation wins our heart, thanksgiving redeems our mind. The battle to be thankful is not a heart battle; it is a head battle–a battle of the mind.

The root word of thanksgiving (thanks) means "to think." It is a verb; it requires action. Your mind is one of the three components of your soul: mind, will and emotions. David, in several Psalms, commands his soul to bless/praise the Lord. He understood the authority he had over his soul to line up with God's truth, victory, promises – his destiny. You have that same power and authority over your soul.

Being a thankful person is a great accomplishment. David said in Psalm 116:17, *I will sacrifice a thank offering to you and call on the name of the Lord.* Sacrifice always costs. Being thankful may cost you your comparisons, your negative thoughts, your anxiety or maybe your depression. It's time to trade up. In seeking an attitude of gratitude and thanksgiving, you rise to a new level of holiness in your life.

The human mind can only hold one thought at a time. It is impossible to hold gratitude and depression... or anger... or fear... in the same thought. It has been said that thankful people cannot be depressed, and depressed people are often not thankful.

ThanksLiving is one of the best things you can do for you. In addition to being good for your spiritual, physical, and mental health, it also positively affects your sleep patterns, self-esteem, and it brings breakthrough. Gratitude can lower blood pressure, improve immune function and improve heart health, including less inflammation and healthier heart rhythms. Thankfulness activates your body's control center (Hypothalamus) that regulates hunger, sleep, body temperature, metabolism, and how the body grows, while it produces Oxytocin, the feel-good hormone. Studies have shown that thankful people tend to experience positive emotions more often. They literally train their "prefrontal cortex" to retain positive information and reject negative stuff over their lives.

Are you thankful? Are you thankful for your present circum-stances? Are you thankful for your salvation, your friendships, your family, your community, your job? Thankfulness is a key that unlocks miracles and turns your situation around because it changes you, your outlook, and your attitude. The strongest heart is a thankful heart. While ThanksLiving may feel like a battle at first, with time and practice you can develop a lifestyle of thankfulness.

Thank God for everything in your life. Thank Him for even the difficulties. He can turn troubles to triumph. *Through Jesus, therefore, let us continually offer to God sacrifice of praise–the fruit of lips that confess his name.* (Hebrews 13:15)

You can amass large amounts of money, have all the latest things, attain reputation, and accomplish great exploits and career accomplishments, but without gratitude it may never feel like it is enough. A thankful heart makes enough, enough.

Don't allow yourself to complain; be very careful to watch your tongue. Instead of complaining, think of ways you can verbally offer God the sacrifice of thanksgiving. Do it for you.

ThanksLiving Begins Today!

Day 1
Thankful for the Day

This is the day that the Lord has made;
let us rejoice today and be glad. Psalm 118:24

Today is a new day–it has never been lived before in all of history. It is full of potential: You get to write your own history. Yesterday is done and gone, tomorrow has not yet begun, but today is yours for the making. What you do with this day is up to you. You can decide to make it great, no matter what. Don't let your history interfere with your destiny. Start your day with Thanksgiving. Psalm 118:24 reminds you that God made this day: therefore, you get to rejoice and be glad in it. Every morning you can thank God for the promise of this new day that has never been lived before.

Each day you begin with a blank canvas. Together, you and God can paint a day that has never been painted before. You choose the colors, the texture, and what you will paint. At day's end you can hang that finished canvas on the wall of your day. Look at it. Give God thanks for what went well. Thank Him for the good things that will come out of what did not feel good. Take ownership of your choices, reactions and responses, and give to God what you had no control over. Invite God to heal those things that caused you to respond poorly or to be angry or afraid. Ask Him to give you the hope, strength and wisdom to do better. Tomorrow will be a new day with a new canvas.

Prayer: "Thank You, God, I woke up! Thank You that today is a new day, a blank canvas, and we will fill it together with miracles that have never been done before! I say "yes" and "thank you" for every blessing, open door, good gift, divine appointment, and miracle You want to do on my behalf today. Help me to see the endless potential within this 24 hours and the power I have to choose what it is going to look like. Today I choose to rejoice and be glad in it! Help me to approach every moment of today with a thankful heart. Help me to be open to the opportunities that lie before me. Let me see, hear and know Your heart for me in a way that unlocks my destiny and creates a miraculous outcome. Heal those things that blind me from hope, and build within me greater faith to know that You are a good God, in a good mood, and that You can turn any situation for good on my behalf. In Jesus' name. Amen."

What do you want to fill your canvas with today?

Day 2
Thankful for What You Have

Let them give thanks to the Lord for His unfailing love and His wonderful deeds for mankind, for He satisfies the thirsty and fills the hungry with good things. Psalm 107:8-9

Being thankful for what you have is a Kingdom key to being satisfied. When you focus on what you have and are thankful for it, what you have is enough. Be thankful for waking up, having a bed, a home, a job, friends, food, and a God who provides for you. Focusing on what you do not have can leave you envious and feeling empty. It has been said that a rich person is not the one who has the most, it is the one who needs the least. Focusing on what you *do* have brings contentment and thankfulness with what you have today.

You may not be a naturally thankful, or a "cup half-full" kind of person. If so, you might want to consider, is that working for you? If you want a fuller, more abundant outcome in your life and relationships you must be willing to operate in a different paradigm than you have been. Doing things the way you always have will get you the results you have always gotten. You will find that being thankful can and will change you–for the better.

When you first open your eyes in the morning, wiggle a toe. Give thanks that you can move it. Move to an ankle or a leg. Can you move it? Be thankful! Can you sit up? Thank you, God. Can you see? Can you hear? Are you breathing on your own? What a great day to give thanks! Do you have food, a job, running water, transportation, a roof over your head? Thank God. A thankful heart helps you have a really good day, regardless of your circumstances. Through gratitude you look at the world very differently. Don't wait until you have the "right" job, house, car, lifestyle or relationship to thank God. Invite Him into today's blessings and invite Him to make them awesome. Even if your circumstances don't change, you will.

Prayer: "Thank You, God, I woke up! Thank You that today is a new day, a blank canvas, and we will fill it together with miracles that have never been done before! I say "yes" and "thank you" for every blessing, open door, good gift, divine appointment, and miracle You want to do on my behalf today. Thank You, God, for _____ (list all the blessings you can think of). Help me not to focus on what I do not have, but instead focus on what I DO have. Thank You, God for the "enough" I have in my life and the abundance that is on its way. Increase my faith and ability to receive every good gift, every open door, every miracle, and every blessing that You have for me today. In Jesus' name, Amen."

What are ten things you have that you are thankful for today?

Day 3
Thankful for the Son

For God so loved the world that He gave His one and only Son, that whoever believes in Him shall not perish but have eternal life. John 3:16

God so loved the world. What a statement. He loved you so much that He wanted to be in relationship with you always and forever. That deserves a thank you. Our thankfulness should start and end with Jesus. Jesus, the creator and eternal Son of God, who lived a sinless life, loves us so much that He died for our sins, took the punishment that we deserve, was buried, and rose from the dead according to the Bible. He gave His life so that we may be reconciled with our Heavenly Father. Thanking God for Jesus, will give you a better understanding of your value and worth to God and to His Son, Jesus. Jesus sacrificed His all for you that you can have not only eternal life, but holiness and abundant life now.

God's heart has always been to be reconciled to mankind. The answer was for Jesus (fully God) to come to Earth, be born into mankind through a woman, so that He (also being fully man) could enter into an eternal Covenant with God on our behalf. It required a perfect, spotless sacrifice to, once and for all, bring forgiveness to man and bring him into eternal relationship with God. Jesus was that pure and perfect sacrifice. Romans 6:23 says, *For the wages of sin is death, but the gift of God is eternal life in Christ Jesus our Lord.* Saying "yes" to Jesus, gives you the gift of eternal life.

Eternity... what a big concept! It is never ending life with the One who loved you so much that He sent His Son to pay the price for you. That means, whatever happens here, no matter how bad it gets, you have eternity to look forward to. The actual covenant is between Jesus and Father God. Because Jesus will never sin, it will be an unbroken covenant from now through eternity; eternal life in relationship with God. All you need to do to be grafted into God's family is to believe in Jesus. That is something to be thankful for. It's what makes your God different than all other gods. God is living and wants relationship with you–His creation.

Prayer: "Thank You, God, I woke up! Thank You that today is a new day, a blank canvas, and we will fill it together with miracles that have never been done before! I say "yes" and "thank you" for every blessing, open door, good gift, divine appointment, and miracle You want to do on my behalf today. Thank You, Jesus, for giving me eternal life; paying the ultimate price and atoning for every sin I have ever done or will ever do. Thank You that because You came to Earth and laid down Your life for me when I was yet a sinner, I never have to be separated from You, Holy Spirit or Father God again. I say "yes" to You and "yes" to eternal life. I receive You as my Savior. Thank You that You love me, like me, and call me Your best idea ever! Come into my heart and fill me with Your truth, love, hope, peace, joy and abundance. In Jesus' name, Amen."

What is God showing you today about thankfulness?

Day 4
Thankful for Love

*Love is patient and kind. Love is not jealous or boastful or
proud or rude. It does not demand its own way.
It is not irritable, and it keeps no record of being wronged.
It does not rejoice about injustice but rejoices whenever the
truth wins out. Love never gives up, never loses faith, is always
hopeful, and endures through every circumstance...
Prophecy and speaking in unknown languages and special
knowledge will become useless. But love will last forever...
Now we see things imperfectly, like puzzling reflections
in a mirror, but then we will see everything with perfect
clarity. All that I know now is partial and incomplete, but then
I will know everything completely, just as God now knows me
completely. Three things will last forever—faith, hope,
and love— and the greatest of these is love.*
1 Corinthians 13:4-13

This is a very famous Bible verse, especially at weddings.
Reading the entirety of 1st Corinthians 13:1-13 will give
you a better understanding of love. In the NIV Bible
"love" is mentioned 590 times, "loved" 93 times, and
other iterations of love another 106 times for a total of
789 times.

Love is a very big deal to God. In fact, it is the nature
of His character and, because you were made in His
image, your basic DNA. The more you operate in love,
the truer you walk according to your identity, and the
simpler things in your life become. Through the power
of love you can overcome even the most difficult life

circumstances. Understanding that love never goes away, but goes into eternity with you, enables you to focus on love here and now. Love opens your life to abundance. It is good to partner with things that last forever – faith, hope and love. And the greatest of these is love.

Prayer: "Thank You, God, I woke up! Thank You that today is a new day, a blank canvas, and we will fill it together with miracles that have never been done before! I say "yes" and "thank you" for every blessing, open door, good gift, divine appointment, and miracle You want to do on my behalf today. Thank You, God, that You ARE love. Therefore, You are patient and kind. You are not jealous, boastful, proud or rude regarding me. You do not demand Your own way with me. You are not irritable with me and You keep no record of my wrongs. You do not rejoice about injustices I may suffer, but rejoice whenever the truth wins out. Thank You, God that You never give up on me, never lose faith in me, are always hopeful about me, and willingly endure through every circumstance with me. Thank You that I can trust You and Your goodness even though I see things imperfectly, like puzzling reflections in a mirror. Thank You that one day I will see everything with perfect clarity and I will know everything completely, just as You now know me completely. Thank you for Your good gifts of faith, hope, and love—and the greatest of these, love. Teach me how to receive the fullness of Your love so that out of my fullness I can pour out greater love to others. In Jesus' name, Amen."

Ask God to show you what He wants to heal so you can love like He loves.

Day 5
Thankful for the Word of God

*All Scripture is inspired by God and is useful to teach us what
is true and to make us realize what is wrong in our lives.
It corrects us when we are wrong and teaches us to do what is
right. God uses it to prepare and equip his people to do every
good work.* 2 Timothy 3:16-17

When you are happy, read the Word of God. When you
are sad, read the Word of God. When you need uplifting,
read the Word of God. When you feel hopeless, read the
Word of God. When you find yourself at odds with the
world, read the Word of God.

God is the Creator of life and He is still creating life today.
The Bible is the only book where the Author shows up
every time you read it. God's number one attribute is
relationship. He never expected you to journey through
life alone. He never leaves you or forsakes you, which
means you are in this life together with Him. In addition
to His presence, He has given you the Bible–full of truth,
direction and Kingdom principles. What you put into
your spirit, soul, and body will determine what comes
out: how you respond to life, and others. God desires
you to know His Word, and to let Him work truth to the
deep places of you, so you can better reflect Him.

There is an old story about a Cherokee teaching his
grandson a lesson about life. "A fight is going on inside
me," He said to the boy, "It is a terrible fight and it is
between two wolves. One is evil–he is anger, envy, sorrow,
regret, greed, arrogance, self-pity, guilt, resentment,
inferiority, lies, false pride, superiority, and ego." He

continued, "The other is good–he is joy, peace, love, hope, serenity, humility, kindness, benevolence, empathy, generosity, truth, compassion, and faith. The same fight is going on inside you – and inside every other person, too." The grandson thought about it for a minute and then asked his grandfather, "Which wolf will win?" He answered, "The one you feed."

Prayer: "Thank You, God, I woke up! Thank You that today is a new day, a blank canvas, and we will fill it together with miracles that have never been done before! I say "yes" and "thank you" for every blessing, open door, good gift, divine appointment, and miracle You want to do on my behalf today.Thank You, God that You have given me truth to feed the joy, peace, love, hope, serenity, humility, kindness, benevolence, empathy, generosity, compassion, and faith within me. Thank You that Your Word is alive and full of power, which makes it active, operative, energizing and effective (Hebrews 4:12, Amplified Bible) to bring me clarity, correction, direction and strategy. Thank You, that every time I read Your Word, You are right there with me. Open my eyes to the things I cannot see. Open my ears to what I cannot hear. Open my mind and life to truths I cannot yet comprehend. Help me to love Your Word and to reflect truth well. In Jesus' name, Amen."

Which wolf have you been more inclined to feed?

Day 6
Thankful for Seasons

There is a time for everything, and a season for every activity under the heavens: a time to be born and a time to die, a time to plant and a time to uproot, a time to kill and a time to heal, a time to tear down and a time to build, a time to weep and a time to laugh, a time to mourn and a time to dance, a time to scatter stones and a time to gather them, a time to embrace and a time to refrain from embracing, a time to search and a time to give up, a time to keep and a time to throw away, a time to tear and a time to mend, a time to be silent and a time to speak, a time to love and a time to hate, a time for war and a time for peace. Ecclesiastes 3:1-8

The Midwest, unlike Southern California, has distinct seasons: Summer is hot and humid, Fall is cool with lots of great color, Winter is cold and gray, and Spring (the start of the cycle) is warm and sunny. The end of any season marks the beginning of a new season. It is important to know that every season ends the good ones and the bad ones. What you learn in each season prepares you to handle the next season. Being thankful for the season you are in allows you to learn quickly the lessons that will help you thrive in both this and the next season.

Every new season of your life will require strength, wisdom, grace, and ability to adapt to that season. It is tempting to want to bring what has worked in the past or the best of last season into a new season. But what fit perfectly in the last season, may be ill-fitting, cumbersome, or ineffective in the new season. God incorporates your experiences, strengths and gifts into what is required of you today, but may be asking you to do things differently. Be open to a change of paradigm. And remember, God never gives you more than you can handle in His strength. That said, R.T. Kendell wrote, "If you are facing a circumstance the likes of which you have never faced before, God is paying you the highest of compliments." So thank God for this season in your life and invite Him to teach you quickly the lessons you need to learn.

Prayer: "Thank You, God, I woke up! Thank You that today is a new day, a blank canvas, and we will fill it together with miracles that have never been done before! I say "yes" and "thank you" for every blessing, open door, good gift, divine appointment, and miracle You want to do on my behalf today.Thank You, God, that there is a perfect time for everything and that no season lasts forever. Help me to move forward bravely, fearlessly and full of hope. Help me to trust Your timing in the seasons of my life, to know that You love me, and are for me. You will never give me more than I can handle in Your strength. Give me faith to know that what is coming will be better than what has been because You are good and I can count on You to provide what I need. Help me to not be stuck or too comfortable in last season's blessings, but to lean into today's grace. I invite You to open the right doors for me and close any doors in my life that hold me back from Your best for me. Thank You that Your love for me, unlike the seasons, never changes. In Jesus' name, Amen."

What have you learned in past seasons that has equipped you for today?

Day 7
Thankful for Sonship

*The Spirit you received does not make you slaves, so that you
live in fear again; rather, the Spirit you received brought about
your adoption to sonship. And by him we cry, 'Abba, Father.'*
Romans 8:15

As a Christian, you are adopted into God's family. To
fully understand the significance of this, let's look at
adoption during New Testament times. Under Roman
law, adoption was used to continue the family line when
there were no natural children. The Romans adopted
adults so that their name would continue. They carried
all the authority of the family name. Romans could
disinherit close family members at any time, but never an
adopted son. God, through the Holy Spirit has adopted
us into His family so that we will continue the line of Jesus
as true sons and daughters. That makes you co-heir with
Jesus–with all the same rights and privileges. It is from
that place of identity and legitimacy you can confidently
live out your birthright and destiny with assurance and
purpose.

You are chosen, loved, unique, wanted. You are God's
child. He chooses you in your uniqueness and you are a
treasure to Him. That understanding of your belonging
enables you to walk in dignity, freedom, honor, and full
legal authority. A child of the King always has access to
their Father, the King, and a place at His banqueting
table. Father God gathers you into His heart and into His
arms... if you let Him. His face smiles upon you and He
is gracious to you, always. The broken choices of those
around you may wound you, but your Father is with you

to heal you, restore you, strengthen you and bless you. Lean into Him today.

Prayer: "Thank You, God, I woke up! Thank You that today is a new day, a blank canvas, and we will fill it together with miracles that have never been done before! I say "yes" and "thank you" for every blessing, open door, good gift, divine appointment, and miracle You want to do on my behalf today. Thank You, God, that I am Your child with full birthright and privileges as a legal co-heir with Jesus. Thank You that I am chosen, loved, unique, wanted and that You see me as a treasure. Thank You for my legitimacy in You and for my adoption into Your family through Jesus' sacrifice. Thank You that my identity is never defined by others' opinions of me, my choices, or my history. I am forever Yours. You are a good Father. You know everything about me. You knew me before I was born. You know the number of hairs on my head. You have seen me on my worst day, yet still choose me and call me Your own. I invite You to bless me, heal me, restore me, and strengthen me. In Jesus' name, Amen."

What is God showing you today about your identity?

Day 8
Thankful for Community

Now to Him who is able to do immeasurably more than all
we ask or imagine, according to His power that is at work
within us, to Him be glory in the church and in Christ
Jesus throughout all generations, for ever and ever! Amen.
Ephesians 3:20

God is three persons, each unique in attribute, yet one body (community). You were created in His image – unique and individual, yet designed to function best in community. We are better together, and with Jesus, we can do more that we can imagine. Being a part of a healthy community is powerful. Jesus modeled that for us when He chose His disciples. He picked people that would not normally hang out with each other and they formed a community that then went out and changed the world.

Community is about sharing, caring, journeying together. However, when you think *your* revelation of God—or politics, or parenting, or anything else—is the only revelation, it leaves no room for others to have a different revelation. It is not that your revelation is necessarily wrong, but that you may not be *completely* right. In that, your challenge will be whether you demand to be right or choose to have relationship. The first leads to division, isolation and rigidness, while those who choose the latter experience growth and healthy community.

If you want to see your community changed, thank God for your neighbors. It is tempting to want God or someone else to fix what is wrong in your community, friends, or family. But we are often called to *be* the change! In John 15:15, Jesus calls us friends—not slaves, workers, cohorts, or companions. Having Jesus as a friend means there is an everlasting bond between us. Through thick and thin, in good and bad, in plenty and want, our friend Jesus will always be with us. That is something to be thankful for; community and friends. Better yet, a community of friends that are centered around Jesus is worthy of thankfulness.

Prayer: "Thank You, God, I woke up! Thank You that today is a new day, a blank canvas, and we will fill it together with miracles that have never been done before! I say "yes" and "thank you" for every blessing, open door, good gift, divine appointment, and miracle You want to do on my behalf today. Thank You, God, that I was created in Your image – unique and individual, yet designed to function best within community. Thank You for my community, my neighbors, my loved ones, my extended family. Give me a grateful heart toward those You have called me to love. Heal the areas of my heart that may want to judge, compare or reject others whose thoughts I don't agree with or like. Help me to celebrate the differences of others and to see in them what You love, what You like, and what You honor. Help me to speak life into the community around me. In Jesus' name, Amen."

What is God encouraging you to be thankful for in your community?

Day 9
Thankful for Leaders

I urge, then, first of all, that petitions, prayers, intercession and thanksgiving be made for all people — for kings and all those in authority, that we may live peaceful and quiet lives in all godliness and holiness. This is good, and pleases God our Savior... 1 Timothy 2:1-3a

If you want the best possible outcome for you, your loved ones, your community, and the world, you must be willing to pray for those God has established in authority or leadership over you. What if you don't like a leader—such as a pastor, boss, or elected official? Or what if you don't agree with their choices or how they lead?

Leadership is a Kingdom model. Everyone submits to someone. Even Jesus did only what He saw the Father doing. How you handle submission and authority is very telling of what is in your heart. David was anointed to be King (1 Samuel 16:13) years before he was actually installed as King. The problem he encountered was with Saul, who actually *was* the King. Saul, tried often to kill David, but was never successful. Maybe you have a boss or a leader that makes your life painful or hellish. David knew that if he were to become King, God would have to make it happen. David refused to lift a sword against God's anointed, Saul, (1 Sam. 35:6; 24:10; 26:9; 26:11; 26:16; 26:23) even when he was close enough to easily kill him. Through that time God worked the "Saul" out of David's heart.

The question for you is this: If you are called to submit to a leader that seems "designed to grind," will you respond in like kind to that leader, or let God work those very things out of your heart? The more you are thankful, the less you complain, the better the outcome—for them and for you. Thank God for the leaders He has given you.

Prayer: "Thank You, God, I woke up! Thank You that today is a new day, a blank canvas, and we will fill it together with miracles that have never been done before! I say "yes" and "thank you" for every blessing, open door, good gift, divine appointment, and miracle You want to do on my behalf today. Thank You, God, for the leaders You have established in my life. Bless them, God, with wisdom, truth, favor, Kingdom strategy and the ability to love those You have called them to lead. Help me to bless those I may not agree with or like. Thank You that You use every situation to teach me, guide me, heal me and make me better... if I let You. Help me to trust You in the midst of my circumstances and know that even if I don't feel the decisions of those who lead me meet my needs or expectations, You can work all things for good on my behalf. Heal those places in me that have been wounded by leaders, so that I will not lead others the way I have been led. And finally, God, show me where You have called me to lead, and give me a heart to lead others with wisdom, kindness, compassion and love. In Jesus' name, Amen."

How has God blessed you through the leaders in your life?

Day 10
Thankful for Forgiveness

When you were dead in your sins and in the uncircumcision of your flesh, God made you alive with Christ. He forgave us all our sins, having canceled the charge of our legal indebtedness, which stood against us and condemned us; He has taken it away, nailing it to the cross. Colossians 2:13-14

Jesus died, paid the price for all your sins and, in the process, forgave you. That forgiveness cost Him everything, but it is a free gift to you. As Jesus freely forgives you, He then calls you to forgive those who have wronged you. *For if you forgive other people when they sin against you, your Heavenly Father will also forgive you. But if you do not forgive others their sins, your Father will not forgive your sins.* (Matthew 6:14-15) Forgiveness is one of the best gifts you can give yourself. Forgiveness is never really about the other person; it is the opportunity to set your imprisoned heart free. Often, you become the things you don't forgive. When you have bitterness and unforgiveness in your heart, it owns you–it consumes you. Until you let go, it will be the filter through which you make all life and relationship decisions. It can be blinding, and crippling. However, you don't have to stay there.

We all know people who have had something bad happen to them years ago, and they continue to be so stuck that it still defines them today. That is not freedom, Jesus came to set the captives free. Carrying unforgiveness is like drinking poison expecting the other person to die. Do you want freedom? It could be time for you to forgive. Forgiving someone *never* means what they did was right or good. God is near the broken hearted. He grieves when you grieve, He cries when you cry. You have never suffered anything alone. While God will not stop the free will of man, there is nothing that has been done to you that God cannot heal... and He wants to heal you.

Prayer: "Thank You, God, I woke up! Thank You that today is a new day, a blank canvas, and we will fill it together with miracles that have never been done before! I say "yes" and "thank you" for every blessing, open door, good gift, divine appointment, and miracle You want to do on my behalf today. Thank You, God, for the gift of forgiveness. Thank You that You have forgiven me for all my sin. Thank You for not holding my bad decisions, wrong choices, and judgments against me. Thank You that the painful, hurtful things that have happened in my life need not define me. Thank You that I can live free today and every day because Jesus paid the ultimate price for all my sin, and the sin of those who have hurt me. Give me a heart to forgive the broken people in my life who have done broken things to me. Help me give my wounds to You, because You, Jesus, paid for them. Heal me, restore me and reconcile my heart so that I will not repeat the cycles that have been done to me. Set my heart free. In Jesus' name, Amen."

Is there anyone God is asking you to forgive? Today is a great day for freedom.

Day 11
Thankful for Supernatural Life

Stretch out your hand to heal and perform signs and wonders through the name of your holy servant Jesus. Acts 4:30

Supernatural is a manifestation or event attributed to some force beyond scientific understanding or the laws of nature. Since Christ—the master and creator of the universe—lives in you, you are not limited to what you can accomplish in your natural strength and ability. You are Super-Natural! Through the supernatural, healing happens, salvation happens, miracles happen. Without the supernatural eternity simply would not be. Your *something* partnered with God's *everything* can accomplish immeasurably more than you can imagine. Within your finiteness you carry the presence of an infinite God. He is with you, in you, and works through you.

Healing is supernatural. Jesus charged the disciples with bringing God's Kingdom to Earth. Luke 9:6 says, *So* [the disciples] *set out and went from village to village, proclaiming the good news and healing people everywhere.* During His life, Jesus healed the sick in spirit, soul, and body, raised the dead back to life. Then He said, *Very truly I tell you, whoever believes in me will do the works I have been doing, and they will do even greater things than these, because I am going to the Father.* That includes you... today! As a believer, Christ has given you the authority to heal, reconcile, forgive and restore. In other words, to do the supernatural! Have you ever prayed for someone to get healed? You can know that every time you pray, something happens. When you pray more, more happens. If you never pray, you will never know. Give it a try.

22

Prayer: "Thank You, God, I woke up! Thank You that today is a new day, a blank canvas, and we will fill it together with miracles that have never been done before! I say "yes" and "thank you" for every blessing, open door, good gift, divine appointment, and miracle You want to do on my behalf today. Thank You, God, for the supernatural. Thank You that I was created in Your image and You are supernatural. Thank You that I am not limited to my natural skills, knowledge, gifts, talents, or resources, but I have power and authority to partner with the miraculous. Show me the truth of my identity and the Kingdom authority I carry as Your child, and as a follower of Jesus Christ. Give me the boldness to step out and pray, believing that You can and will bring healing and miracles. I invite You to do the miraculous in me and through me. Thank You, God, that You only want good for me, and that includes supernatural favor over my life. I say "yes" to the supernatural miracles You have for me, and the miracles You want to do for others through me today. In Jesus' name, Amen."

In what areas would you like to step more fully into the supernatural?

Day 12
Thankful for Creation

In the beginning God created the heavens and the earth.
Genesis 1:1

In the beginning, God created... you... mankind... the heavens and the earth. His creation is still going on today. There are objects in the universe so distant you cannot see them with the most powerful telescope, and objects so minute you cannot see them with the strongest microscope. Consider how your body parts all work together uniquely, yet in orchestration. Each cell is designed with specific purpose and function... so it is with all creation. Is it possible to look at what God has created and not be awestruck by His order, creative power, and sense of humor? (Have you seen the platypus?)

Your world is full of color, texture, beauty, and mystery! When was the last time you stepped outside to watch a sunrise, sunset, or stopped to smell the fresh air after a rain? Being thankful for creation allows you to see all His creation with appreciative eyes: not only the natural things, like trees, mountains, oceans, lakes, and wildlife, but also God's greatest creation—mankind. You will naturally adopt a spirit of thankfulness for anything you take time to appreciate. That being said, you will never be able to enjoy the treasure of those things which you are not willing to look at in wonderment. Gratitude opens your eyes to see more, in fuller color.

Genesis 1:17 reminds you that you were created in God's image, all mankind was. There are more than 7 1/2 billion iterations of what God looks like reflected in the people just living today. Each one carries a different facet of God's limitless creativity and *all* are necessary to create an accurate mosaic of God's image. Who you were created to be, your unique design, and your circle of influence is different than every other person in the world, and that is to be celebrated. When you can be thankful and celebrate yourself as a gift God gave to the world, you will be better able to give thanks for others… and for all His creation.

Prayer: "Thank You, God, I woke up! Thank You that today is a new day, a blank canvas, and we will fill it together with miracles that have never been done before! I say "yes" and "thank you" for every blessing, open door, good gift, divine appointment, and miracle You want to do on my behalf today. Help me to be thankful for what You have created. Open my eyes to the beauty of people, places and things all around me. Thank You for not only creating, but for loving the world still. Help me never again take for granted the air I breathe, the grass I walk on, the rain, plants or diversity of people and animals. Open my eyes to the wonder and color all around me. Point out the miracles of life I used to look past or discount. Remind me to take time to look at a sunset and know that at the end of every day is the birth and hope of a new day. Thank You, God, for the revelation of You in all of creation. In Jesus' name, Amen."

List ten things you are thankful God has created in you.

Day 13
Thankful for Breakthrough

That same gospel is bearing fruit and making new growth the whole world over, as it does among you and has done since the day when you heard of God's grace and learned what it truly is.
Colossians 1:6 (REB)

Be thankful that as a child of the most-high God, you are destined for breakthrough in your life. Like the seasons, you and your circumstances are always changing. Remember, nothing lasts forever. Jesus, in John 16:33, reminds you ...*In this world you will have trouble. But take heart! I have overcome the world.* Right before that, Jesus says He is telling you this so you can have peace. You never have to be afraid when you come up against obstacles. Jesus wants you to know that every time you hit a wall, or come against a barrier, you can look for and expect a breakthrough. Further, each time you have a breakthrough, not only do you grow, but everyone around you gets to walk in a new level of freedom.

Breaking through may cost you the comfort of staying stuck, or a misbelief about you, others or God. However, freedom is your prize! When you are on the other side of your challenge, be sure to thank God that you made it, He was with you, for the things you learned, and how you have grown stronger because of the very resistance that tried to hold you back. Romans 12:21 encourages you, *Do not be overcome by evil, but overcome evil with good.* The power of good will always overcome evil.

When seeds are planted, they first grow roots. The roots grow downward to make the plant stable and to support growth. Once these roots take hold, a small shoot will begin to break through the soil. You can plant a seed and it can look like nothing is happening for a long time, but under the earth that seed is preparing to support the breakthrough and growth that is beginning. It can seem that way for you too, like nothing is happening, changing, or getting better. Sometimes when you feel the farthest from breakthrough, you are the closest. Jesus strengthens you to face life's obstacles and overcome them. You can do all things through Christ, who strengthens you. (Philippians 4:13)

Prayer: "Thank You, God, I woke up! Thank You that today is a new day, a blank canvas, and we will fill it together with miracles that have never been done before! I say "yes" and "thank you" for every blessing, open door, good gift, divine appointment, and miracle You want to do on my behalf today. Thank You, God, that You are the author of breakthrough. Thank You for promising me peace even in the midst of the trials and tribulations of my life. Thank You that I am not defined by what comes before me, but forever strengthened by my breakthroughs. Thank You that I never need fear the walls in my life and that I can lean into You to help me break through. Thank You, Jesus, that You are greater than anything that would oppose me, and that in You, I can do all things. Make me brave. Make me fearless. Strengthen me. Give me the wisdom I need to press through discouragement, unbelief and doubt. Thank You, God, for breakthrough. In Jesus' name, Amen."

What breakthrough are you contending for in your life?

Day 14
Thankful for Creativity

And afterward, I will pour out my Spirit on all people. Your sons and daughters will prophesy, your old men will dream dreams, your young men will see visions. Even on my servants, both men and women, I will pour out my Spirit in those days.
Joel 2:28-29

Without dreams you would not be reading this book. Without dreams you would not currently be sitting on a chair, a couch, or at a desk. These things would not exist without the dreams of people who were willing to turn them into reality. Dreams make the future possible. You were designed in God's image with creative ability to *call those things which are not as though they are.* (Romans 4:17) You were wired to be able to receive Kingdom revelation for strategy and invention that has never been done. Supernatural innovation, discovery, progress and passion lay within the hearts and minds of those who dream with God. Without dreams, paintings would not be painted, sculptures would not be sculpted, buildings would not be built, vaccines would not be discovered, and airplanes would not exist. Thank God for dreams.

"Every dream begins with a dreamer. Always remember, you have within you the strength, the patience, and the passion to reach for the stars and change the world."
-Harriet Tubman

Dreaming is contemplating the possibility of doing something, often that which has not been done before. Here is a dreaming exercise for you to do. Take a moment and settle into a comfortable chair. Close your eyes and clear your mind of the activity of the day. Get quiet on the inside. Now, ask yourself this question: "If I had all the resources in the world and could not fail, what would I do?" Think big. In fact, think outrageously big! What would you do? Who would you affect? Who would benefit? How would you feel? How big is the impact? Where would it be? How would the world be better? Remember to think as large and outside the box as you can. Now, close your eyes again and dream *bigger*! Then, close your eyes and dream *bigger than that*! Your God is capable of even that last dream.

Prayer: "Thank You, God, I woke up! Thank You that today is a new day, a blank canvas, and we will fill it together with miracles that have never been done before! I say "yes" and "thank you" for every blessing, open door, good gift, divine appointment, and miracle You want to do on my behalf today. Thank You, God, for creativity and for dreams. Thank You for my ability to dream God-sized dreams that are so much bigger than what I can do alone. Give me the faith to believe that You love me enough give me big dreams in my heart, then give me the ability to accomplish them. Thank You, God, that You still create, and You invite me to create with You. In Jesus' name, Amen."

What dream has God given you that needs to be dusted off?

Day 15
Thankful for Grace

*There is no difference between Jew and Gentile, for all have
sinned and fall short of the glory of God, and all are
justified freely by His grace through the redemption that
came by Christ Jesus.* Romans 3:22b

Grace is the free and unmerited favor of God, even when
we haven't earned it and don't deserve it. Grace extends
kindness to the unworthy. In the New Testament, grace
refers to God's love in action toward men who deserved
the opposite of love. Grace came to Earth in the form of
God's only Son, Jesus, who died on the cross, descended
to Hell, and now sits at the right hand of the Father,
interceding on our behalf. He who was sinless paid for
all our sins, in full, once and for all. *God made Him who
had no sin to be sin for us, so that in Him we might become the
righteousness of God.* (2 Corinthians 5:22) Because of that,
we will never get the punishment we deserve. Instead, we
are given eternal life, love and reconciliation with God.
That is amazing grace!

Ephesians 2:8-10 says, *For it is by grace that you have been
saved, through faith – and this is not from yourselves, it is the
gift of God – not by works so that no one can boast. For we are
God's handiwork, created in Christ Jesus to do good works, which
God prepared in advance for us to do.*

This concept of grace seems counter-intuitive to our
American culture, which has little grace. We expect
people to be held accountable, to work hard and earn
what they have. We insist on equality, fairness and justice.
Now, these things are not necessarily wrong or bad, but

they are not grace. Unmerited grace is like someone just randomly paying off your entire mortgage. The debt may be in your name, but because it has been paid in full, you will never have to make another mortgage payment and the house is yours! That is unearned favor. Grace brings you redemption even though you do not deserve it. The grace that Jesus freely gives you brings you into alignment with God. Thank Jesus for undeserved grace.

Prayer: "Thank You, God, I woke up! Thank You that today is a new day, a blank canvas, and we will fill it together with miracles that have never been done before! I say "yes" and "thank you" for every blessing, open door, good gift, divine appointment, and miracle You want to do on my behalf today. Thank You, God, that because Jesus died for my sins, I will never get what I deserve. Instead I will receive unmerited favor and grace. Thank You, God, that Your love for me is a free gift and in endless supply, so it will never run out. Help me to take the grace You extend to me and pour it out generously to those around me... even those I don't agree with. Make me a conduit of Your healing, miracle-working grace. In Jesus' name, Amen."

Where is God challenging you to give grace?

Day 16
Thankful for Mercy

But because of His great love for us, God, who is rich in mercy, made us alive with Christ, even when we were dead in our transgressions. Ephesians 2:4-5

Mercy and grace have similar meanings, but they are not the same. Grace is God blessing us despite the fact that we do not deserve it. Mercy is God not punishing us as our sins deserve. Romans 3:23-25 reminds us that we have all sinned and deserve Gods judgment. God, the Father, sent His only Son to satisfy that judgment for those who believe in Him. As God treats us with mercy we do not deserve, He then calls us to deal with others with the same mercy.

God wants you to be generous with mercy, so you can receive generous mercy. How you treat/give to others will determine what you receive. Luke 6:37 says, *Do not judge, and you will not be judged. Do not condemn and you will not be condemned. Forgive and you will be forgiven.* Why? James 2:13 answers, *For judgment without mercy will be shown to anyone who has not been merciful. Mercy triumphs over judgment.* The "Be" Attitudes in Matthew encourage you to be merciful, so you will be shown mercy. That is what Proverbs 11:17 is talking about when it says, *The merciful man does himself good, But the cruel man does himself harm.*

What does mercy look like in today's world? The parent who forgives the drunk driver who killed their child. If *anyone* deserves to demand judgment and refuse to render mercy it would be a parent whose child's life was stolen, or anyone who has suffered loss through a senseless crime. However, God calls each one of us instead to forgive and extend mercy. Not for their sake, for OUR sake. He knows that unforgiveness, anger and bitterness consume our thoughts and eat us up from the inside. True freedom can only come by laying our pain at the feet of Jesus (who paid for all sin) and extending forgiveness and mercy to those who have wronged us, and our loved ones. God loves you and extends mercy to you for no other reason other than His love. He gives mercy so you can move forward in life when you, or others, have messed up. Because of God's mercy, you are able to come into His presence and be healed. That is reason to give thanks.

Prayer: "Thank You, God, I woke up! Thank You that today is a new day, a blank canvas, and we will fill it together with miracles that have never been done before! I say "yes" and "thank you" for every blessing, open door, good gift, divine appointment, and miracle You want to do on my behalf today. Thank You for Your great love for me and that because of Your mercy I am alive with Christ, even when I was dead in my transgressions. Help me to treat others with that same mercy You extend to me, and to lay my judgments at Your feet. Thank You that I don't have to stay stuck; I can give You my pain from those who have wronged me and You will heal my broken heart and restore me. I invite You to do that in any unhealed area of my life. Thank You, God, that You are merciful... ALL the time. In Jesus' name, Amen."

When has God shown you mercy?

Day 17
Thankful for Hope

May the God of hope fill you with all joy and peace as you trust in Him, so that you may overflow with hope by the power of the Holy Spirit. Romans 15:13

Hope is that feeling of expectation and desire for a certain thing to happen, a feeling of trust. Our hope in God is confidence that what God says will happen, will happen. Jesus brings abundant hope: enough that you can have hope every day, in all things. Hope comes from knowing that something good is about to happen, something great is around the corner, someone will do the right thing, and that God's love is greater than any other force. In receiving hope, carrying it and giving it away, hope changes and fills the atmosphere around you with hope itself.

Holy Spirit gives us hope for the times we do not see God working, or when He seems to be working in a way we don't understand or like. Christians often say, "God is Good, all the time." That is true. But what about the times it doesn't feel like He is good? Usually it is when we cannot see the good He is doing on our behalf, or are blocking His blessing with our judgments.

There is a story about an old couple driving down a country road. The man was driving, the woman was settled against the passenger door. The woman said, "Pa, you remember when we used to drive down this road all snuggled together?" Her husband replied, "Ma, I ain't moved." God has not moved. And when you feel distance between you and Him, don't stay there, move closer.

34

When you lean into God, you will find the hope of Him in everything. Hope is one of the three things that will last forever, according to 1 Corinthians 13:13. Paul, in Romans 5:5, says hope does not disappoint us. Does that mean that everything will go the way you want, when you want, with whom you want? No. What can you Hope in then? Hope in God's presence. God is always with you; He will bring you through the difficult times, will redeem all things, and is able to heal you from the wounds of this imperfect world. Hope because Jesus sits at the right hand of the Father, interceding on your behalf, and has given you supernatural authority to change the atmosphere of whatever challenges you are facing.

Prayer: "Thank You, God, I woke up! Thank You that today is a new day, a blank canvas, and we will fill it together with miracles that have never been done before! I say "yes" and "thank you" for every blessing, open door, good gift, divine appointment, and miracle You want to do on my behalf today. Thank You, God, for the hope that is in You that I can access at any time. Thank You, that You are greater than my circumstances and that You have my back. Thank You that hope is in limitless supply and always mine for the asking. Thank You that my hope is not determined by my circumstances or my resources. Thank You, God, for hope. In Jesus' name, Amen."

Where does God want to give you hope today?

Day 18
Thankful for Joy

You will show me the path of life; in Your presence is the fullness of joy, at Your right hand are pleasures for evermore.
Psalm 16:11

You have shown me the paths of life; Your presence will fill me with joy. Acts 2:28

Joy is a feeling that is more than happy or glad and is not determined by our circumstances. It can be the quiet, inner sense of well being, and it can also be an abounding feeling of elation that comes when we are filled with the Holy Spirit. Both flow from a deep abiding relationship with Jesus. Nehemiah 8:10 reminds us that the Joy of the Lord is (your) strength. It can keep, propel, and empower you to endure hardship. Joy comes with understanding that God takes delight in you and is always with you and for you, no matter what. When you have that understanding, you can look past circumstances and find joy in everything.

If Christians carry the power to bring God's transformation into their circumstances, why do so many live a joyless existence? What does God say about joy? In John 17, Jesus prays to the Father for us, that we might have His joy fulfilled in us. That is what He wants for us, God's joy, not just when things are going well, but always, in all things. In Matthew 25:21 God says, *"...you have been faithful over a few things; I will make you ruler over many things: enter into the joy of the Lord."* This requires you to enter in. Joy is a daily decision and can be a battle. Luke 6:23 encourages you to *leap for joy – when you are hungry, when*

36

men reproach you, when they cast your name as evil... rejoice in that day and leap for joy. In Psalm 30 David assures us that God can turn our mourning into dancing. The key is to rejoice! Thank God for everything! It is a choice. It is your choice. Will you let your circumstances dictate whether or not you can have a joy-filled day? Or will you invite God to fill you with a joy that makes no sense in the face of your circumstances? You decide. Being joyful makes gratitude easier.

Prayer: "Thank You, God, I woke up! Thank You that today is a new day, a blank canvas, and we will fill it together with miracles that have never been done before! I say "yes" and "thank you" for every blessing, open door, good gift, divine appointment, and miracle You want to do on my behalf today. Thank You, God, for joy. Thank You that joy is for the asking and the receiving. Thank You for the power of joy in my life to break through stress, sadness, grief, unbelief, darkness, depression, destruction, hopelessness, and even death! I say, "yes!" to new measures of joy in my life today! Teach me how to live in joy and to give it away freely to others. In Jesus' name, Amen."

Where do you need more joy in your life today?

Day 19
Thankful for Peace

Peace is my parting gift to You, My own peace, such as the world cannot give. Set your troubled hearts at rest, and banish your fears. John 14:27

Peace is one of the names of God, (Jehovah-Shalom), and therefore, speaks to the nature of God. The Hebrew word for peace, *shalom,* comes from a root denoting wholeness or completeness. It is most commonly used in the Bible to refer to a state of well-being, tranquility, prosperity, and security. Jesus gave shalom to His disciples at His farewell (John 14:27), and He is still giving peace to you today.

Peace is not the absence of war, but the presence of God. In fact, you usually don't need peace unless conflict is happening or possible. Peace does not rely on understanding, but comes from knowing who God is and knowing that He can do what He says He can do on your behalf. Peace is the assurance that God will be with you in every circumstance and He will provide what you need, when you need it. Being thankful for peace requires trusting God's nature and timing and being at peace with both.

Have you ever had something that you really wanted to happen, not happen? Did you later realize that it would have not been good if everything happened when you wanted it to? Maybe you wouldn't have found that *better* job, or a *bigger* pay raise, or the *better* house on a *better* street if you had gotten the one you wanted?

38

In Philippians 4:6, Paul says, *Do not be anxious about anything. But in every situation, by prayer and petition, with thanksgiving, present your requests to God. And the peace of God, which transcends all understanding, will guard your hearts and your minds in Christ Jesus.* In every situation, you can have peace. It is a promise – Jesus will guard your heart and mind with peace. The key is presenting your request to God, with thanksgiving. ThanksLiving creates gratitude, which generates contentment, which causes peace.

Prayer: "Thank You, God, I woke up! Thank You that today is a new day, a blank canvas, and we will fill it together with miracles that have never been done before! I say "yes" and "thank you" for every blessing, open door, good gift, divine appointment, and miracle You want to do on my behalf today. Thank You, God, for peace. Thank You that You are always with me, and where You are, peace is. Thank You that peace is not determined by my circumstances and that I don't even have to fully understand peace to receive it. I invite You to heal any broken places in me, to restore the things that have been taken from me, and to fill me with abundant peace to overflowing. In Jesus' name, Amen."

In what areas of your life would you like more peace?

Day 20
Thankful for Victory

The Lord your God accompanies you to fight for you against your enemy and give you the victory. Deuteronomy 20:4

O Death, where is your victory? O Death, where is your sting?' The sting of death is sin, and sin gains its power from the law. But thanks be to God! He gives us victory through our Lord Jesus Christ. 1 Corinthians 15:55

For to love God is to keep His commands; and these are not burdensome, because every child of God overcomes the world. Now, the victory by which the world is overcome is our faith, for who is victor over the world but he who believes that Jesus is the Son of God? 1 John 5:3

Many have asked, "What does the victorious church look like?" It looks like you! Often people think the victorious church is the "perfect" body of believers... without any issues. By definition, victory is an act of defeating or overcoming an enemy or opponent in a battle. Which means the victorious church is one that is still fighting. We should be proud of our scars; they are proof that we have survived our battles and overcome what the world has thrown at us. When people see our scars, instead of being ashamed of them, we should point at them and say, "That is when God did this for me." Or, "This is what I learned about me and about God." Or, "This is what I have overcome and I am not afraid. Let me pray for you because if God did it for me, He will do it for you."

When fighting for victory over thoughts, feelings, mindsets or addictions, it is important to know that victory doesn't mean you will never be tempted. Instead, victory is not giving in to the temptation, now. For example, being tempted to smoke is not the same as smoking. The victory is not smoking in the moment when you are tempted. Will you do it perfectly? Maybe not. Micah 7:8 says, *Do not gloat over me, my enemy! Though I have fallen, I will rise. Though I sit in darkness, the LORD will be my light.* If you stumble or fall, just don't stay there. That is victory!

Prayer: "Thank You, God, I woke up! Thank You that today is a new day, a blank canvas, and we will fill it together with miracles that have never been done before! I say "yes" and "thank you" for every blessing, open door, good gift, divine appointment, and miracle You want to do on my behalf today. Thank You, God, for victory. Thank You, Jesus, that You have overcome and are Victor over the world, including the fight I am in today. Thank You that I am the head and not the tail; and victory can be mine, in You. Thank You that You go before me to win the battle. Thank You that I have never fought by myself, You have always been with me. Thank You God, for victory. In Jesus' name, Amen."

Count your victories. What have you had victory over in your life?

Day 21
Thankful for More

Now to Him who is able through the power which is at work among us to do immeasurably more than all we can ask or conceive, to Him be glory in the church and in Christ Jesus from generation to generation for evermore! Amen.
Ephesians 3:20 (REB)

Jesus can do for you more than you can even ask or conceive, and He wants to! You can be so content having just enough, that you don't ask for the more. Daily bread is great, and something to be thankful for, but God wants to bless His kids with more! In Matthew 25:29, Jesus promises that whoever has will be given more. Christ died for that more. Romans 5:10 says, *For if, when we were God's enemies, we were reconciled to Him through the death of His Son, how much more, now that we have been reconciled, shall we be saved by His life!* Jesus says, in John 10:10b-11, *I came that they may have life and have it abundantly. I am the Good Shepherd. The Good Shepherd lays down His life for the sheep.* God wants you to have so much more than just eternal life, He wants you to have the more that comes with His presence now.

The key to more begins with thankfulness. Jesus models this when He fed the five thousand. It was after He gave thanks that the food multiplied to meet the need before Him. *But He (Jesus) said to His disciples, "Have them sit down in groups of about fifty each." The disciples did so, and everyone sat down. Taking the five loaves and the two fish and looking up to Heaven, He gave thanks and broke them. Then He gave them to the disciples to distribute to the people. They all ate and*

42

were satisfied, and the disciples picked up twelve basketfuls of broken pieces that were left over. Luke 9:14-17

The more thankful you are, the more thankful you become. The more hopeful you are, the more you are filled with hope. When you experience joy, you can always have more. When Jesus promised to give you more abundant life, the promise is more. Because God and His resources are without limit or end, you never have to be content in yesterday's blessings. Today can be the day for *your* more: life, peace, joy and more of God. It is all for the asking. So thank God for what you have, and ask for the MORE!

Prayer: "Thank You, God, I woke up! Thank You that today is a new day, a blank canvas, and we will fill it together with miracles that have never been done before! I say "yes" and "thank you" for every blessing, open door, good gift, divine appointment, and miracle You want to do on my behalf today. Thank You, God, that You can do immeasurably more than I can even image, and You want to. Thank You that You and Your resources are limitless, so I never have to be satisfied in yesterday's blessings. Today I ask for more life, more peace, more joy, more hope, and more of Your presence. Today I ask for the more: those things I know I need and even those things I do not know I need. In Jesus' name, Amen."

In what areas of your life are you asking God for more?

Today is the first day of the rest of your life. Choose ThanksLiving!

Acknowledgments

We want to acknowledge and thank those who have helped this book become more than a concept. First, thank you to our kids, grandkids, and extended family who have journeyed with us through our broken places and always been gracious as the test group.

Thank you, Pastors Matthew and Siobhan Oliver, for the assignment... and for always encouraging us to dream.

Thank you to Kelsey White for designing the cover, to Kiley Oliver and Deb Hollis, who pulled this book out of a grammatical abyss, and to Neal Hollis for crafty formatting.

We are greatly supported by our friends and family at The Family Church, who continue to listen to and encourage our teaching. What a gift... thank you.

And for you. Thank you for investing in our dream.

Printed in Great Britain
by Amazon